Con$umer

Wi$e

*If **only** we had listened*

Edited by Valerie Hockert

Valerie Hockert
CollProf@aol.com

Table of Contents

Introduction

This is a collection of articles as originally published in Con$umer Wi$e. Volume 1 was as newsletter and later became a column in Today's Family magazine.

These articles **amazingly** hold a lot of merit today.

If only more of us had read these and followed the suggestions to be *consumer wise*... perhaps we'd be better off today....

--Valerie Hockert

Volume 1 No. 1

Seven Ways to Save $$$$ When Shopping

By Laureen Mercier

Whether you're the main consumer in your household or an occasional shopper, these tips can save you money.

1.   **Think Before You Spend.** When heading out to make a purchase or to just browse, take along a pen and paper. Write down information such as: color, price, brand, and where you saw the article. Take this information and comparison shop at other stores. Then go home and think over your purchase. You may even change your mind about the purchase altogether.

2. **Plastic Savings:** Never spend more on your credit cards than you will be able to pay off in full when the bill arrives. The biggest mistake most people make is to

purchase a sale item on their credit card knowing full well they won't be able to pay for it when the bill arrives. So what has happened? You have lost your savings to credit charges. Most times your big sale item costs you more than the full price.

3. **Group Shopping:** You shop together, so why not buy together? Before buying that new kitchen appliance or new car, talk to everyone you know. If you're lucky, you can find a small group of people who are interested in your purchase. Once your group has agreed on the product, go to the manager and ask for a group discount. Most managers will give at least 10% off when making a large sale.

4. **Where Does it All Go?** Keep a spending record. It's the little things that kill even the best thought-out budget. Write down everything you buy—from a package of gum to that single postage stamp. After a

month, you should be able to see why your budget is not working.

5. **Bulk Up:** Whenever a most used food (or other used item) goes on sale, buy it by the case. This way your savings will last until the next big sale. If you can't find an item on sale ask your store personnel about case discounts. Some stores will give you a discount just for buying the whole case.

6. **Cutting Coupons May Cost You:** Coupon savings are great, but watch your brands. If the coupon is not for your regular brand, you may end up spending more. Always check your prices before using coupons to make sure your savings really are saving you money.

7. **How Much Does it Really Cost?:** Mail order has taken over our mailboxes, and in

some cases our common sense. The prices look good on the surface, but remember to add in the shipping and handling before signing that check. That little $1.98 item may cost you $4.98once all the hidden costs are added on.

Money and How to Keep It

By Doris B. Gill

Pay Yourself First. Save at least ten percent of your pay before you spend a dime or pay a bill. Consider this payment as one of your obligations. As the account grows fatter, like a porker ready for market, you'll be getting further from the "buy on credit," quicksand mire.

Open a Money Market Savings Account. A brokerage account will pay higher interest than most banks, and there's safety in it too. Transfer only enough money into your bank checking as needed for that month. Keep as much money earning interest for you as you can.

Pay Bills at the Last Minute. As bills are received, make out checks, but don't mail them. Note due date, and post payments about five days before. Write the mail date in the upper right hand corner (which the stamp will later cover). For example, a bill

arrives on 6/22 and is due 7/12. The mail date is 7/7.
Place the envelopes in a conspicuous place so you'll
mail them on time. (My payments are placed in a wall
basket by the front door.) On the mail date, affix a
stamp and send. Although you have deducted the
payment amount from your checkbook, your money is
earning interest for extra days, and it adds up!

Did You Know…?

…that outlet malls are especially popular these days? They are a Mecca for shoppers and offer a wide variety of merchandise at good prices. Sometimes these prices can be so good—and so tempting—that we buy much more than we need. Did you really need to go in the crystal store and get a set of eight Santa goblets? You're only going to use those four weeks of every year….

--Deborah Wilson

…that you can cut down on your dry cleaning bills? Don't take your clothes to be dry-cleaned just because they're wrinkled. Opt for "press only," or better yet, iron them yourself.

--Jonathan Pond

…that July is the second best month to buy an air conditioner on sale? (February is the best.)

--Con$umer Wi$e

...that you could probably buy two roundtrip airline tickets (one for your departure, and one for your return) cheaper than to pay the regular round-trip airfare? Check it out....

--Con$umer Wi$e

...that the Rule of 72 tells you how long it takes your money to double? You divide the number 72 by the interest rate you're getting. If you're getting six percent, it takes 12 years to double. 72 divided by six equals 12. If you're earning eight percent, it takes nine years to double, since 72 divided by eight is nine.

--Les Abromovitz

The Art of Frugality

By Darrin Koltow

Here are some ideas for painting the town, without emptying your paint bucket.

Join an "entertainment" club. By using coupons or membership cards, club members get discounts to activities as varied as dining out and miniature golf.

When considering a play or movie, go to matinees instead of shows in the evening and other prime times. Don't buy theater tickets from places in shopping malls, they get the best seats, but ask a sleep price for them.

Choose the real stars over celluloid ones. On a hot summer's night, drive to the outskirts of town, park the car, spread a blanket on the hood or the ground, and enjoy the charms of a starlit sky. Make a game of identifying constellations. If you don't know the standard ones, make your own. After you've made several, try to discern the first one. Create your own movies by putting your constellation characters in scenarios.

Do the same with clouds during the day No Clouds? Pack a lunch and some earplugs—cotton is a more inexpensive alternative—to a local airport and watch the planes soar.

Use your library regularly. You may be surprised at its cornucopia of resources. Many libraries, besides having the latest novels, magazines, and newspapers, have popular videos to rent for a minimal cost.

By photocopying old newspapers, you can give someone a blast from the past by showing him/her the current events at the time of his/her birth. The newspapers are kept on microfilm, which you can browse through with easy-to-use machines. The machines also let you photocopy the newsprint. Fair-sized libraries have microfilm for many different newspapers. Once you've tried newspapers, use magazines. People, especially adults, get a big kick from seeing the cars and clothes that were in vogue years ago. At about ten cents per page, you can give more pages of yours than the paltry publication of this sort that gift shops sell.

Check the library's bulletin board for more low-or-no-cost fun. Your library may have meeting rooms where intriguing local clubs gather. You can also hear recitals, and fiction or poetry readings in such rooms.

While you're in the library, pick up a do-it-yourself book. Learn to fix furniture, cars, plumbing, and just about anything else. Even if you don't fix anything, you can use the knowledge you gain to assess the workmanship of others.

For another education forum, take a class offered by the local adult education program. Courses are inexpensive, and you can learn everything from gardening to speaking another language. Such classes are often taught by people who are employed in the subject he/she is teaching.

Thus, he/she may be more "in touch" with the subject than a formally certified teacher would be.

The best way to save money is to view frugality not as a chore, but as an art. Paint your world with a palette of your own thrifty ideas.

The Best Buy Quiz Book
By Rich Latta

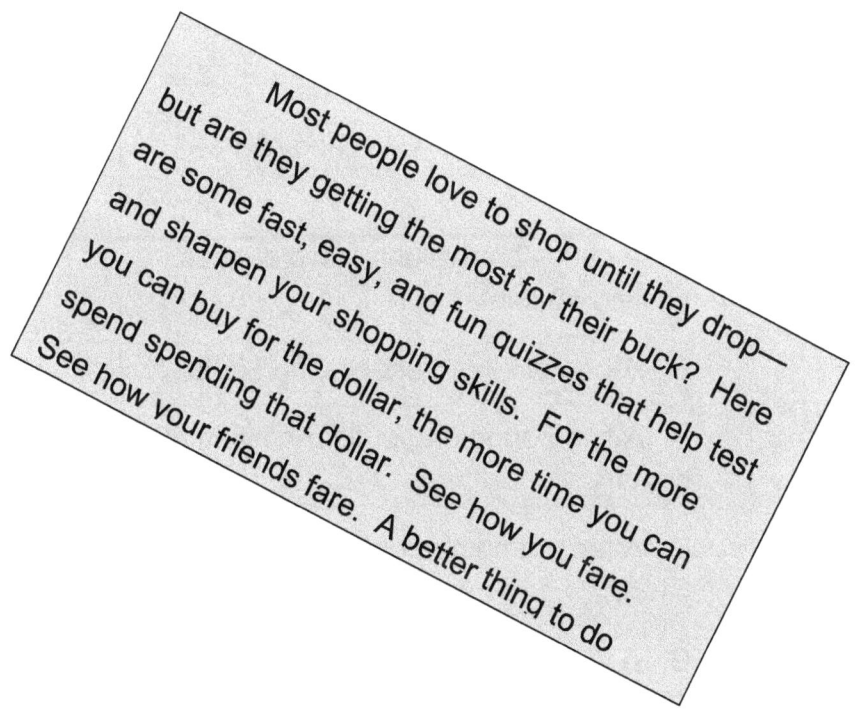

Most people love to shop until they drop—but are they getting the most for their buck? Here are some fast, easy, and fun quizzes that help test and sharpen your shopping skills. For the more you can buy for the dollar, the more time you can spend spending that dollar. See how you fare. See how your friends fare. A better thing to do

Rank these from the best buy to the work buy:

1.   A. Ten oranges for two dollars. Oranges weight two ounces.

B. Oranges at 80 cents a pound.

C. A bag of three pounds of oranges for $1.80

2.   A, A pound of bite size candy bars costing $2.49

B. A candy bar weighing two ounces costing 40 cents

C. A bag of eight bars costing $2.99

3.   A. A five-pound bag of flour costing 89 cents

B. A ten pound bag of flour costing $1.80

C. A 25 pound bag of flour costing $3.99

Answers: 1. C, B, A; 2. A, C, B; 3. C, A, B

Know the Language When You're Shopping

By Bobbe Quinlan

Legend has it that all women know about shopping. That's right up there with the legend that all men are mechanically inclined. But, like modern cars, shopping has become so complicated that it takes some study to gain the knowledge to be a smart shopper. One of the things the smart shopper must know is the "language" of advertising. Here are some hints to help you as you pore over the newspaper ads. (Source: The Savvy Shopper by Judy Y. Ocho and Larry Goodman.)

Up to 50% Off—it sounds impressive, but since the ad does not give the minimum percentages, the chances are that most of the merchandise listed will have a substantially lower percentage off.

No Prices Listed—60% off is not enough information for the smart shopper. Unless you know the store and its usual price line, you have no idea whether 50% off is a good buy.

Bait and Switch—if you find an article priced well below the price you'd expect to pay, changes are you won't be able to buy it when you get to the store. Either they will be "out" of the item, or the sale item will be so cheap looking the salesman will start pointing out the defects and attempt to sell you a higher priced item.

Sold Elsewhere For…--where is the "elsewhere?"

Giveaway Prices—Ridiculous Prices—Crazy Prices—stores are not in the business of giving merchandise away. When faced with an ad like this, do some comparison shopping. You may find some bargains at ridiculous prices, but you may also find cheap merchandise at cheap prices.

Exaggeration—watch out for the ad that makes liberal use of superlatives—"amazing, fantastic, unbelievable." If it seems too cheap to you, you're probably right to suspect the merchandise. It may turn out to be undersized, in "peculiar" colors, or of poor quality.

Artwork—drawings and photos will typically be chosen to show the merchandise at its best advantage. A dress, for instance, will probably not fit you the way it fits in the pictured ad. Remember the garment has been fussed over, pinned and straightened for hours before the picture was taken. This can make a rag look like a Paris creation.

Two-fers—do your arithmetic before you decide on buying a two-fer. Also, compare ads at other stores. If one store has pillows on sale at two for $20.00, and another store has them at $9.00 each, obviously the second store has the better price. Also, many stores are reluctant to sell a single item at its sale price if you don't really want to buy two.

Truckload Sales—don't be thrown by big numbers in these type sales. You only want *one* so it doesn't matter how many they have to sell. The numbers to watch for are assortment numbers—32 patterns, 40 styles, etc.

Beware the Asterisk—the asterisk (*) or other symbols can conceal unwelcome news for the buyer. However, they can also be good news. If the star tells you "No Returns," "No Delivery," etc., it is a signal that the values could be special because the store cannot afford "frills" at the sale prices.

In other cases, that little star could end up costing you more than you intended to pay, or covers up hidden costs. "Batteries not included" is the classic case.

The little star can also indicate exclusions or limited assortments. This is normal at the end of the season sales.

"Assembly required:" is a phrase that can strike terror in the hearts of many shoppers. Look for this star when buying toys, furniture, etc.

"Plus installation" can also produce unpleasant surprises to the unwary shopper. It applies not only to carpeting, but to large appliances. You may find that a washer bought at a sale price does not include the plumbing connections. These parts plus the installation could raise the cost considerably higher than the sale price.

"Not at all stores" and "Ask for warranty" are also starred subjects in many ads. Smart shoppers will read the small print and watch for the stars.

By learning the language of advertising and really *reading* the ads you find in the daily papers, you can save both money and time. The bargains are out there—all a smart shopper has to do is learn the language and learn how to find them.

Volume 1 No. 2

Secrets of the Smart Shopper

By Lisa Morell

In an era where economic uncertainty is a fact of life, the importance of saving money for a rainy day cannot be underestimated. These days, the onus is on all of us to try to stretch our dollars as far as we can.

An obvious place to start cutting costs is the grocery bill. Due to the cut-throat competitive nature of the food business, the biggest disservice the penny conscious consumer can do for his grocery bill is to go to the same supermarket and mindlessly buy the same items week after week.

The astute shopper is well aware of the glaring discrepancies and the frequent fluctuations in the prices of basic food staples and household supplies among the major supermarkets. Unfortunately, it feels like consumers are inundated with flyers.

The process of smart shopping can be divided into two discrete stages; preparation and the actual shopping. The importance of planning ahead by doing your homework before you shop cannot be overemphasized. First, you should wait until all of the flyers have arrived. Then you should review all of the flyers looking for things you normally buy on sale and discard the rest. You should also check your coupons to see if you have any coupons for anything that is already on sale. Magically, this can multiply your savings, sometimes allowing you to buy certain items for prices that are so low they are ridiculous. Imagine a bottle of shampoo for 22 cents!

The second way the smart shopper plans ahead is by buying in bulk In the beginning until the cupboards become well stocked, this may require a small cash investment. Eventually, you will find that your grocery bills will actually decrease. The beauty of buying the items that you would normally buy, in bulk, such as toothpaste, juice, ketchup, is that you are able to make a considerable savings without feeling any corresponding sacrifice. After all, what difference does it make to you if your brand toothpaste costs 99 cents or 44 cents?

When actually shopping, do not be afraid to go to more than one store, especially in urban areas where competing stores are usually located in close proximity. The smart shopper scorns the consumer complacency bred by store and brand loyalty. From experience, I can assure you that for the most part there is little difference among brands. I would invite anyone who would disagree to think of the savings in terms of vacation money, and then ask themselves whether they really care what kind of toilet paper they use at home when they are sunning themselves on some tropical island in March. I often buy cheaper brands and put them in the containers of brands certain members of my family respect, and have yet to be caught at my tricks. This is an old trick restaurants have been using for years!

Finally, try to avoid shopping *without* a list—or when you are hungry. Impulse buying isn't necessarily a bad thing, but try to make wise choices. Don't hesitate to take advantage of in-store specials when you are sure the price is right, and that you will use the item. Be wary of what I call the "fake" in-store special, where the sign says "special" but the price isn't any lower than usual. I am confident that with a little planning and ingenuity, every consumer can realize a savings on their grocery bill. Don't be a complacent consumer!

Did You Know…?

...that miles are dollar guzzlers? Set aside one day to run errands, map out your itinerary, and make a loop. Your last stop should be the stop closest home. My product loyalty ends at the gas pump. I watch for the best price on gasoline and if I'm at quarter tank, I fill up where the price is good. We all know how much gas prices fluctuate, but be wary of whether they are cheaper in the city or country. As a rule, there is more pricing competition in areas where there are more service stations (the city).

--Deborah Wilson

...that a quick oil change is cheaper in the city? A quick oil change in my town (pop. 23,000) charges $25. Just 20 minutes away is a community, four times as large. I can pick up a copy of their free circulation weekly paper and find two to three ads for auto service and invariably one will have an oil change as low as $9.95. Over the course of four oil changes a year this adds up to a savings of almost $60.

--*Deborah Wilson*

…that travel insurance often duplicates coverage in homeowners or health insurance policies? The homeowners policy may cover lost or stolen baggage. Your health insurance often gives you sufficient medical coverage. As a result, you may only need the trip cancelation/interruption coverage in the travel insurance policy. If your airline and hotel tickets are fully refundable, you may not need travel insurance at all.

--*Les Abromovitz*

…that if you're taking a cruise, the cancellation fee waiver is often a better option than travel insurance? Most waivers let you cancel for any reason, as long as you notify the cruise line at least a day before the ship leaves port. On the other hand, most travel insurance policies only reimburse you, if you cancel for a particular reason such as the death of a close relative.

--Les Abromovitz

Style for Less

By Lynn Baldwin

Are you tired of wasting hours combing discount store clothing racks for bargains? Do you wish you could take advantage of department store convenience and service without paying top dollar? With the following tips, you can dress in department-store style at discount prices.

1. **Shop often.** Gone are the days of once-a-year sales. In today's economy, nobody can afford to pay full price, *and you don't have to.* Stores have responded to the "I won't buy it unless it's on sale" mentality with frequent sales and markdowns. Shopping often in your favorite department store will keep you abreast of these trends, as well as giving you the opportunity to "keep your eye on" a particular outfit until it's at a price you can afford.

2. **Get a store credit card.** This advice may at first seem unwise—everyone knows the danger of an out-of-control credit card. However, if your department store credit card is used wisely and paid off at the end of the month, it can help you save money in two ways: (1) Advance sales notice Many stores mail their credit card holders advance notice of sales events. Some also include money-off coupons, which makes sales even more enticing. (2) Opening discount. Many department stores offer a discount, often 10-15% on *all* purchases made the day you open a store credit card account. Especially when used in conjunction with sales, this could signify substantial savings.

3. **Shop off-season.** Although it's difficult to think swimwear when it's snowing outside, off-season shopping can be a bargain hunter's delight. Department stores need to clear out merchandise at the end of one season to make room for the next—so they

mark it down, down, down, in hopes of getting rid of it.

4. **Part-time job.** Department store salespeople generally receive a 20-25% discount throughout the store, on both regular and sale-price merchandise. Department stores offer part-time hours which are convenient for someone wanting a second job, those who only want to work evenings and weekends, and anyone who loves good clothes at great prices!

Save Money in No Time

By Robynn Clairday

Yes, I want to save money—but not at the expense of my busy schedule. One major weakness of some money saving tips is that they are too time-consuming. How long does it take to separate all of those two-ply toilet tissues into separate double stacks? Money-saving tips often involve using a lot of space. Where are you supposed to stack those 50-pound bags of flour, especially if you live in a condo or apartment? I have found small ways to cut costs and save money without wasting time or space.

- Join a credit union, even if this means joining an organization. Credit unions through employers or other groups offer economical banking. Save on banking charges (check cashing, deposits, withdrawals, etc.)

- Use electronic withdrawals and deposits. Save on various charges and postage. Real saving is avoiding late charges on bills.

- Make minor adjustments to your thermostat; lower the temperature a few degrees in the winter and raise it in the summer.

- Buy day-old bread and pastries at grocery stores and bakeries. They often sell them at half-off and usually it tastes fine. If a little state, a brief zap by the microwave usually freshens them up.

- Most grocery stores show price per unit of their products. Check actual savings when using coupons or buying them on sale.

- Grocery stores often place the most expensive products at eye level. Look up and below for the bargains.

- If you have a local farmer or gardener, ask for produce at season's peak for cheapest prices.

- Buy clothes out of season.

- Usually flea markets and garage sales offer better bargains than resale shops. Go to flea markets and garage sales right before closing time, even though goods are often picked over. Eager sellers are ripe for bargaining.

- When running errands during the weekday in the city, find a nearby pay phone to call a local friend for only 25 cents. Phones are often deserted. Local same area code calls have become expensive.

- Use beauty supply stores for beauty products. Samples are often the best buys.

- Add water to cat or dog dry food, and make your own moist food. It's much cheaper than manufactured canned or moist pet food.

- Barter for expensive auto and appliance repairs. Check around neighborhood and with friends. Exchange cooking, cleaning, sewing, or other talents for repairs. Bartering is subject to taxation.

- Dilute shampoo with a little water; it lasts longer.

- Air dry clothes instead of using the dryer. Clothes look new longer.

- Put an egg timer near the phone or set the timer on your microwave. This is very helpful for keeping long distance telephone calls in check.

- Longer, blunt haircuts need fewer trimmings. Perhaps you could cut back on the frequency of haircuts.

Cost-Saving Alternatives for Travel Plans

By Margo Isbell & Kathleen Eyman

With summer in full swing, many families are searching for vacation options that will offer them the most for their money while staying within their travel budgets. As a result, vacationing families are finding it more important than ever to look for cost-saving lodging alternatives that allow them to keep more of their travel dollars to spend on dining and entertainment.

One lodging option that is often overlooked by family travelers is extended-stay hotels, which offer extra space and value-added amenities, and are located near key attractions in their area. These apartment-style hotels—which were originally designed to cater to business travelers—are attracting a growing segment of leisure travelers by offering prices that are competitive with traditional hotels, and providing far more space and a variety of home-like amenities that are appealing to families traveling on a budget.

Consider for example, the benefits offered by hotels such as Homewood Suites, a leading extended-stay hotel chain.:

- dining areas, fully equipped kitchen, refrigerators, stoves, coffee-makers.
- television, videocassette players, sleeper sofa, ceiling fans.
- swimming pool, sports court, exercise center, barbecue grill, convenience store, laundry facilities
- complimentary breakfast and social hour

In addition to the variety of amenities and services that typically are provided at extended-day hotels, Homewood Suites, also provides another key advantage to traveling families—its 100% satisfaction guarantee. Simply stated, the guarantee assures guests that they will be completely satisfied, or their night's stay is free.

As consumers look for ways to shave travel costs without sacrificing their family vacations, cost-effective alternatives like extended-stay hotels will become smart lodging choices among the leisure traveling public. And saving money on these travel basics will enable families to concentrate on the real vacations priority—*having fun without spending a fortune.*

Volume 1 No. 3

Saving Recession $$$$
By Doris B Gill

It's tough to stretch pay checks in normal times, but during our current recession, it almost takes a magician to cover basic necessities. If you're taking a pay cut, facing a layoff, or if you're just frustrated by inflation and higher taxes, you know the importance of making every penny count.

Small changes add up to big dollars.

Share subscriptions. If you absolutely can't afford your own, consider sharing newspaper and magazine subscriptions with a neighbor. Take weekly or monthly turns being first, then pass them on.

Recycle greeting cards. It's a shame not to use colorful cards more than once. If an envelope is needed, make one.

Extend felt pen life. When writing becomes faint, add a few drops of water or food coloring to the opposite end of pen tip. Remove the cap and drip liquid into the pen.

Use cloth napkins. Invest in launder able finger wipers. Use daily, and erase paper ones from your grocery list for good.

Sharpen scissors. Hone scissors by cutting through fine sandpaper once or twice.

Extend sandpaper life. Moisten the reverse side with water. The abrasive will be more flexible and last longer.

Recycle garden hoses. A worn out hose can start a new life as a soaker. Carefully punch uniform holes with an ice pick.

Repair screens. Wipe of brush small holes with transparent glue.

Restring beads. Use dental floss—it's stronger.

Save lipsticks. Old or unwanted colors can be used as an undercoat or as a lip protector.

Sleep in old sweat clothes. Save stained, torn sweat pants and tops—they make toasty winter sleepwear. Mend the holes—tops and bottoms don't have to match. When painting or doing messy jobs, sweat clothes are the perfect attire.

Extend panty hose life. Wear gloves when donning them.

Make your own stain pretreating solution. Add to a one-quart spray bottle; 1 cup dishwashing detergent, 1 cup ammonia, 1 cup water. Spray stained garments before pacing in automatic washer.

Make window cleaner. Add an 8 oz. spray bottle; 3 tablespoons ammonia, 1 tablespoon vinegar, and fill with water.

Save suds. Place bar soap on a sponge. No soap will be wasted as you use the sudsy "dish" as a wash cloth. Collect hotel soap on your next trip. Wet, and mold into larger bars.

Heat less beverage water. Heat only ½ to ¾ cup of water for tea or instant coffee. Add cold water to the brewed drink, which will be just right for drinking.

Switch off oven early. Turn off heat five or ten minutes before done time. Bake at night to help heat the house in winter, and keep it cooler during sizzling, summer days.

Turn down thermostats. You can be quite comfortable at 68 degrees. Wear extra sweaters and two pair of heavy socks.

Shut off unneeded lights. Last one leaving a room switches off bulbs. Charge a nickel to forgetters.

Did You Know…?

…that coupons are amazing? I will never again growl at the person in front of me at the checkout lane with a laundry list of coupons. That person is now me! And through careful attention to the ads, clipping coupons and redeeming only at stores that double coupons, our family has cut 30% of its total grocery bill! Watch the ads!

--*Deborah Wilson*

…that there are outlet stores for every interest, from fishing to lingerie, to toys, kitchen appliances, children's clothing (a Grandma's downfall), t-shirts, and brand name outlets? Treat the outlet stores like a trip to Las Vegas—very carefully. Tell yourself ahead of time what you will spend. Leave your credit cards at home. Take a limited number of checks and a maximum amount of cash. You don't have to spend it all, you know.

--*Deborah Wilson*

…that buying gold jewelry isn't the same as investing in gold? Although the gold content of the jewelry has some bearing on its price, you're paying more for the artistic labor that went into it. Furthermore, since gold is a soft metal, it's often mixed with base metals to make jewelry. Worse yet, some jewelry only has gold electroplate on it which is just a coating.

--Les Abromovitz

…that your library may have books on cassette tape that you can check out and use in your car? If you're in the car a great deal, these can be advantageous. Since these audio books are expensive to buy, there's another option. In some parts of the country, stores are opening which rent these audio tapes at a reasonable price. If you must purchase them, inquire if friends and relatives are interested in swapping tapes.

--Les Abromovitz

How to Start Investing

By Janice A. Telford

Today's low interest rates on bank account and money market funds have caused millions of Americans to take a broader look at the world of investments.

If you are just getting started in investing, most financial advisors agree that you should follow a few basic steps.

1. Determine your financial objectives. There are many reasons for investing. Some of the most common include: earning more current income; building your net worth; saving for a home, college education for children or your retirement; and reducing your tax burden.

    Each of these objectives suggests different investment strategies and different types of investments. For example, if you want more current income, you might do better with a fixed income investment, such as a bond, rather than a growth company stock.

2. Understand your current financial position. Calculate your net worth by adding up all of your assets (value of your home, personal property, investments, bank accounts, pension/profit-sharing plans, etc.) and then subtract your liabilities (money you owe for such things as mortgages, car loans, credit card debt and other bills).

    If most of your assets are in real estate (which is true for many people), you may need to convert your investments to cash on emergency. Therefore, you may not want to invent in long-term instruments. However, if you have assets that can be converted easily to cash (e.g. money market funds or stocks), you might want to invest longer-term for a higher return.

Similarly, you should calculate an annual household budget by adding up all of your income for the year (salary, interest and dividends on investments, distributions by pension/profit-sharing plans, alimony) and then subtracting your regular, essential expenses (mortgage or rent payments, food, utilities, clothing, etc.) The balance is the amount you have to spend on personal uses.

3. Understand your tolerance for risk. Most investments have some measure of inherent risk. If you have sufficient assets and income, you might be willing to accept greater risk in exchange for a potentially larger gain. However, if you cannot afford to lose your investment principal, you probably should consider such low-risk investments which, while relatively safe, usually do not earn a high return.

4. Understand your investment. Before you invest, you should understand how the

investment works. If, for example, you want to buy the common stock of a company, take the time to learn about the company and the industry in which it operates by reading the company's annual report or an analyst's research report.

Likewise, a mutual fund may seem to be a simple investment because your money will be managed by professionals. However, you should know such things as the fund's performance over the short and long-term compared with that of other funds, the investment objectives and strategy (what the fund invests in stocks, government bonds, tax-free bonds, etc.), and what your costs will be to invest or withdraw your money. These questions usually are answered in the fund prospectus.

5. Seek professional advice. As briefly outlined above, there are many things you should know before your invest. An experience4d financial advisor can help you

at every step—from helping you set financial goals, to explaining various investments to helping you monitor the success of your account.

To You and Your Car

By Carlos Piovanetti

Ours is an automobile dependent society. We rely on our cars to drive the kids to school, get to and from work, and go to the supermarket. Remember, the last time that your trusted four-wheeled friend let you down, and how much it cost you to get her going again. With a bit of preventive maintenance, we can save money on repairs and that dreaded phone call to the mechanic. Consider the following:

- The thread on the tires are worn out and must be replaced. Buy bargain tires marked blems. They are just as good as brand new tires except for minor cosmetic blemishes on the side walls.

- The rubber on the windshield-wiper blades is dry and the blades are not cleaning properly. By rubbing the edges with a knife you can lengthen the life of the windshield-wiper. This exposes the softer material underneath, improving the wiping ability of the blades. Do not use wipers to clear snow and ice from the windshield, as the rubber will tear leading to poor visibility in bad weather. Use a plastic ice scrapper.

- Turn on the air conditioner for ten minutes every week, even during the winter. This will maintain coolant pressure and avoid costly breakdowns.

- Keep battery terminals corrosion-free. Using a wire brush or steel wool, scrape battery posts and cable clamps. Mix baking soda with water and clean the top surface of the battery. Make sure that the solution does not seep under cell caps.

- Never wash the car's finish with hot water. Instead, preserve the finish by washing it with cold or lukewarm water.

- Protect it from acid rain. Wash frequently, adding one tablespoon of baking soda for every gallon of water. Rub your hand along the finish; if it feels rough get it waxed and polished.

- Check the oil level once a week. If checked by a gas station attendant, make sure the dipstick is inserted all the way. It's been reported that some attendants will show you the dipstick indicating that the car is low on oil, then use an empty can and make believe that they're added a quart of oil. Add oil whenever the dipstick is below the full mark.

• Oil additives by and large are of no benefit to the engine and may cause damage or faster engine wear. It is best not to use them. However, if you insist on using them, make sure the additive is approved by the manufacturer and will not void the engine warranty.

Using preventive maintenance techniques will increase the longevity and performance of a car. Sooner or later a trip to the mechanic is inevitable. It is a good sign if the mechanic is certified by the National Institute of Auto Service Excellence, particularly for the repair needed. Better yet, get a written estimate and compare it with another mechanic.

It's a good idea to start a "car repair" fund by saving a few dollars weekly. This way, when the inevitable occurs, there will be fund set aside to cover the expense or most of it.

Vacation Lodging on a Tight Budget

By Susan Leahy

Is your family on a travel budget? Would you like to save money on vacation lodgings? Inexpensive overnight opportunities exist for the adventuresome traveler to glitzy cities or pastoral countryside, from Bed & Breakfasts to lakeside cottages. With a little imagination and investigation, you can stay in great places at affordable rates and save money at the same time.

Go to college. Many colleges and universities offer dormitory rooms during school breaks. From Iowa cornfields to Arizona desserts, college locations scatter across the United States. Some schools maintain overseas campuses in cities like London and Paris. Call the main campus housing office for details.

Explore elder/youth hostels: Sometimes rustic hostels aren't for everyone. But, the cost is low and you'll meet interesting people from all over the world. Check travel guide books for hostel addresses and telephone numbers.

Travel off-season. Vacation at fabulous resorts directly before or after peak season. Make reservations early and enjoy considerable savings, sometimes up to half off the regular rates.

Rent a condo. Call the local Chamber of Commerce for condo rental information. Convenient for groups of four to eight people, families or friends can jointly pool economic resources and ease travel budgets.

Buy your breakfast. Steeped in charm and character, Bed & Breakfast establishments are often luxurious, private homes whose proprietors love company. Reasonable rates include overly large breakfast and comfortable overnight lodgings for budget-conscious guests.

Request a discount. Hotel reservation agents rarely volunteer discount information, but, lower room rates are routinely available for the asking. Be sure to inquire about reduced tariffs when arranging hotel or motel lodging.

Balance your budget hotel. If you spend little time in your room on vacation, consider a budget hotel or motel. Several national motel chains feature a network of comfortable, but not fancy, rooms in various locations from big cities to out-of-the-way places for travelers on a budget.

If you can stand it. If your lodging budget is near zero, stay with friends and relatives or camp out. Better still, vacation near home. Take day trips. Tour nearby sites you always planned to visit but never have, or stay at home and enjoy the cheapest vacation lodging available—your own bed!

Volume 1 No. 4

Give Yourself a Little Credit

By Kelly B. Sagert

A candy-apple red Thunderbird, a college education and your own business—what do they have in common? Most people need a loan to finance any of those. To get a loan, you need a great job and a lot of money, right? Wrong! One of the most important requirements for a loan is good credit.

It's never too early to start establishing good credit. Maybe you have enough money to start your business, but what if it is time to expand? Plan ahead.

What exactly is good credit? As James Rieth, a financial expert put it, "Your credit is an accumulation of your present and past bill paying habits." Banks report your payment pattern to a credit bureau The credit bureau, in turn, issues its findings to institutions when you ask them for new credit.

A common requirement for loan approval is two years of good credit. Catch 22! To get a loan, you need good credit, but to get good credit, you need a loan How can you get started?

Open a savings account at the bank of your choice. A local institution may be a better choice, since you can sometimes deal directly with the underwriter who approves your loan. Put a portion of your earnings in the savings account, and leave it there. A pattern of good savings is looked upon favorably by banks.

Next, ask your bank if you can borrow against your savings account. This procedure is granted automatically in most cases. You will usually be charged 2-4% higher in interest than you earn. The savings balance is frozen, and you can generally ask for fairly flexible repayment terms.

If you have saved $500, you may be able to borrow 90% of it, or $450. Open a savings account at another bank with that money. Withdraw your loan payment each month until the loan is paid off. Ask for a letter stating that you have paid off your loan as requested, since these types of loans are often not reported to the credit bureau. Note that you have now established a relationship with two banks.

Repeat the process again. Borrow from the second bank, and deposit it in a third bank. Many loan applications ask for three bank references, and now you have them.

Armed with your references, apply for a VISA or MasterCard. Often a new borrower will be granted a limit of $250. Use this bank card carefully, without overspending. Don't pay the balance off in one month, however. Pay it off in two installments, so that the bank will report the payments to the credit bureau.

Don't be discouraged if you are refused credit. Try all three institutions; if this doesn't work, ask a relative to be a co-signer. The co-signer fills out the application with you, and will guarantee prompt payments.

If ever you cannot make a payment on time, call the bank ahead of time. Banks would rather come up with an alternative payment plan than to continually contact you for a missing payment. Protect your credit at all costs. Poor credit can prevent you from being granted a car loan. Late payments show up on your credit report for seven long years.

If you already have a poor credit rating, call the credit bureau immediately. They will allow you to write a brief explanation, and they will attach it to each copy of the credit report that goes out.

So set your sights on that million dollar business, but start setting your credit foundations today!

Did You Know...?

...that in today's society, making the most of your income is becoming a necessity. As job insecurity increases, benefits change, and corporate mergers change management structure, the future is only as far away as the next payday.

--Deborah Wilson

...how much you spend in two weeks? Track your expenses, then have a review of your budget. Did you really need to order pizza two nights last week? What about that fast food lunch? A salad and a piece of fruit would have been better. You went to the movie on Saturday night and paid top dollar? If you insist on seeing a movie try the twilight hour or Sunday matinee, usually about half price or even better—check the local listings and find a neighborhood matinee where that particular movie is playing.

--Deborah Wilson

…that you can save money on disability insurance? Lengthen the elimination period which is akin to a deductible. Opt for a 90-day waiting period instead of 30 days, which is much more expensive.

--Les Abromovitz

…that many grocery stores now accept credit cards? Although this may be convenient, it's a bad idea if you don't pay your credit card balance in full when it comes due. If you don't, you'll be paying interest charges on your groceries. Because of that extra cost, your food order won't be much of a bargain. Furthermore, it's often a sign of credit problems if you need to change necessities.

--Les Abromovitz

Five ways the Stay-at-Home Mom Can Make Extra Money Now!

By Margaret-Mary Jaeger

Like most moms who stay at home, I chose to do so in order to spend as much time with my young child as possible before she goes out into the world, begins a life of her own, and forgets about me. My husband earns enough money that I am afforded this luxury. Even though I don't go out into the work force each morning and earn a salary, my days are still energetic and busy ones. I, like many stay-at-home moms, have learned to utilize my free time productively. Without the stress and strain of the work place to overload me, I have discovered a few ways in which to make some fast, easy, extra money by using my home as my work place.

1. *Coupons.* Most moms wouldn't dream of going to the grocery store without their little cache of manufacturer's coupons tucked safely within the confines of their purse. I

haven't paid full price for a box of cereal or a can of coffee in ten years! If you routinely use the coupons provided free in the Sunday or daily papers, and you genuinely need and use the products, then this is an excellent way to make a few extra bucks. Say you have ten item coupons totaling $6.98 in savings. Now, most of us either pay by cash or check and delight in the savings earned. But what if you took that $6.98 and stashed it away somewhere, forgotten? If you do this every time you go shopping—place the amount saved in an envelope or a cookie jar—you'll be surprised at how much you'll have in a few months' time. I routinely save $10-$15 a week on coupons, but even if you save $3-$4 a week, that's over $150 a year! And what a delight when the stores honor double coupons.

2. *Sell clothes on consignment.* We all have clothes in the back of our closets that will never feel our bodies next to them again. A dress whose size we no longer are; a coat

that survived three good winters. More and more consignment shops are popping up—stores that will take your clothes and try to sell them for you. The rules are pretty general; the clothes must be in good condition, clean, and buttons and zippers must be intact. Most consignment dealers will take more than ten pieces of clothing at a time, and they'll tag them and decide on the price. The usual split of the money earned is 50/50. So if you bring in a dress that you paid $100 for, the consigned cost will be anywhere between 25 and 60% of the original cost. That means you'll get roughly $27for it. It may not sound like a lot, but it's only one item. Multiply that out for a few items, and the cost can be considerable. And—the shop owner does all the work for you, and you get paid!

3. *Crafts.* Many moms have the innate ability to be able to sew a Halloween costume together with only a few days warning. Some can take a cut-out pattern and an hour later have a stuffed Santa or a

Thanksgiving turkey pillow for their efforts. If you're this type of mom, get the sewing machine threaded, because you can rake in big money doing seasonal crafts. Fabric stores have pre-printed cut-out patterns of everything from Christmas mice, to Halloween witches, to Easter baskets for sale. The cost is minimal. You can sew up a lot of holiday items and then invite your friends in for a home showing. Many women do not have the time, the talent, or even the inclination to sew craft items. This is why sellers at craft fairs make so much money. The public is hungry for handmade, homemade items, especially of the holiday sort. Or if you quilt of needlepoint, you can make money selling those items also.

4. *Type term papers.* Remember what it was like when you were in college, and you had all your reading and studying to do, plus term papers? I was in college during the time the personal computer was still in the embryo stage, so my papers were hacked

away on a portable automatic typewriter. Well, people today still need their papers typed, and many just don't have the time, or the computer to do them. If you like to type and can find the time between naps, hockey games and ballet lessons, then this is an excellent way to make extra money. Place an ad in the newspaper or put a flyer on the student union bulletin board. If you get three or four papers to type, each 15-20 pages, you can ear, well, figure it out…

5. *Organize kid's parties.* My daughter's friends love to come to her birthday parties because we always have a new and exciting theme surrounding them. Last year, we had a costume party where very kid could dress up like their favorite cartoon movie character. The parties revolve around a main theme. For instance, my daughter adores the *Little Mermaid,* so one year we had an under-the-sea mermaid party, complete with crab cake cookies, and yellow flounder-aide. If you're creative, you can really help out moms who aren't and

who dread organizing kid's parties. You charge a one-time fee for the day, and then you're in a charge, working within the budget the parents offer you. It's not only a good way to earn some extra money, it's also very rewarding and fulfilling to have a child thank you for the wonderful party!

Getting the Most from Your Coupons

By Helen F. Brassel and Fred M. Brassel

If I told you that last week I paid 19 cents for a pound of margarine, got a bottle of salad dressing free, or that a manufacturer paid me 35 cents to use their steak sauce, you'd probably say "Where can I find a store like that"? The answer: "Right in your neighborhood."

Couponing can save you between $10 and $20 each week in return for a few minutes of coupon clipping. Refunding can save you even more—free products for the price of a postage stamp. Last year, Americans redeemed 7.05 billion coupons, and estimates of maximum savings range from $400-$1000 annually.

Here's a how-to system that only requires about an hour a week of my time. It squeezes every penny out of the coupons, and the savings can buy a lot of cookies for the kids.

How to find the coupons and refund forms.
Newspapers are the best source, particularly the Sunday paper, which usually has small booklets of coupons and forms. Women's magazines are another good source with coupons and forms printed on the magazine page as part of the advertisement. Coupons and forms also come in the mail, sometimes with a free sample. To ensure a continuing supply of coupons via these home mailers, fill out and return the questionnaires you get in these packets. Manufacturers also will insert a coupon for form right in the package, or print one on the outside. Store bulletin boards will sometimes have coupons or refund forms tacked to them.

How to pay only 19 cents for margarine.
Recently, a major producer of butter introduced a new margarine and provided $0.50 coupons in the Sunday paper inserts. By watching for a sale at the store, which ran a week later, the margarine was $1.19 instead of the usual $1.69. The sale saved me $0.50 and the doubled coupon saved me $1.00 more. The result—a pound of margarine for $0.19.

How to get products free. One way to reap this benefit is the traditional "Buy one, get one free" offer. Another way combines coupons and sales. Remember, shopping in a store that doubles your coupons will enable you to cash in on these "freebies." Say, for instance, your supermarket flier has salad dressing on sale for $0.99 and you have a coupon for $0.50. The doubling policy of the store makes the coupon worth $1.00. When you combine these two savings in a store that has a sale and gives double coupons, too, you really come out ahead. You get the product free, or they actually pay you $0.01 to use it. A mayonnaise company may give you a coupon for a free head of lettuce or a salad dressing company a coupon for a free package of tomatoes.

How to get most out of your coupons:

- Plan you menus
- Make a shopping list
- Match coupons to list
- Check the advertising flyer for sale times
- Use manufacturer's coupons on specials

- Combine store and manufacturer's coupons

Volume 1 No. 5

10 Ways to Have Fun Without Spending All Your Cash

By Emily Sarah LIneback

Are you tired of hearing about the expanding economy while your pocketbook continues to be skinny? Or maybe you're bored with doing the same things again and again. Limited funds don't mean limited fun. Don't get depressed—get creative!

1. **Rent a movie.** Instead of paying $5-9 per ticket, plus snacks, skip the theater and stop by the video store. You can enjoy an old classic or a recent release complete with your own munchies for only a few bucks

2. **Grace a museum.** Some historical and science museums don't charge admission or occasionally offer special rates, and there's always a new exhibit to see. Spend an afternoon finding out more about the special exhibit your local museum is hosting.

3. **Rummage through a salvage yard.**
   Suddenly your junk drawer won't seem so
   overwhelming, and you're likely to discover
   some extraordinary deals.

4. **Attend a seminar.** Libraries, community
   organizations, and churches sometimes
   hold free seminars. Register for a
   genealogy class, family enrichment clinic or
   crafts workshop. Enjoy the fellowship,
   refreshments and learn something, too.

5. **Visit a farm.** Ever petted a cow? Find a
   farm and mingle with the barnyard animals.
   If it's okay with the owner, take oranges for
   the horses. Wear old shoes and have a
   wholesome time.

6. **Have a BYOD party.** Have each guest or
   couple bring an assignment dish. Decide if
   it will be a "grown-up" party just for the
   adults or if children will be included, too—
   with a "side" party all their own. It's an
   entertaining evening for everyone with little
   cost to anyone.

7. **Go to a flea market.** Along with antiques and whatnots, new things abound. And kids will love prices that make their allowances go further.

8. **Watch for free events.** Catch a benefit symphony concert or go to a play performance where admission is a can of food for charity. You get a night of culture *and* help others.

9. **Explore "uncharted" territory.** Hop in the car and drive down roads where you've never been. Enjoy the scenery and note stores or spots where you'd like to return.

10. **Visit a rest home of a hospital.** Go see a friend, relative, or residents you don't know. Take old books and magazines to leave for them to enjoy. Sing, play an instrument, or simply listen. Everyone has a story to tell. And sharing our time with others is one of the greatest gifts we can ever give.

These are only ten of an endless list of possible outings and events (that could very well turn into family rituals!) where the main ingredients are a dash of time and at most only a sprinkle of money.

The times we remember most involve not necessarily lots of cash, but a piece of ourselves. So try out these enriching outings, then construct your own list of fun, unique, low-cost activities to do alone and with your family. You will be the richer for it!

Did You Know…?

…that you can get more from buying stock than just a good return on your investment? Many companies offer perks to shareholders. Marriott shareholders can get discounts on room rates. Tandy gives a discount at its Radio Shack stores. Nonetheless, never select a stock just because you get some perks by buying it.

--*Les Abromovitz*

…that if you rent a car, the agent may offer a fuel option which looks good at first glance only? The rental car agent will stress that you'll pay less than the going rate for gasoline, as long as you bring the tank back empty. Unless you drive the last few miles on fumes, you'll usually bring the car back with several gallons in the tank. Therefore, it usually pays for you to take the fuel option which requires that the car be brought back with a full tank.

--*Les Abromovitz*

...that saving money or economizing is not new? Everybody does it. Remember the pioneer woman who used her egg money for extra household items? My mother used to save S&H Green Stamps. It took a drawer full of those little books, but we got many household items that way. My first spice rack was courtesy of Betty Crocker proof-of-purchase points. The nice thing about those programs was you could set a goal and see tangible evidence of your savings.

--Deborah Wilson

...that one of the problems we all share is that spending money feels good, and when we want something; we want it now? But if you can postpone both gratifications, chances are the item will still be there—on sale. You can save a lot of money over the years if you recognize that the item you so desperately want to purchase now will probably go on sale in the end.

--Jonathan Pond

Ways to Save Money Traveling By Air

By Sharon Tabor Warren

If your option for travel is to fly, there will be an expense of time spent checking fares, but the savings in dollars can make the end result well worth it. Check air fares early and every way possible: contact a travel agent and get the lowest quote; call each airline available to you (the agent can tell you who flies to your destination) and get their quote; check the travel sections of Sunday papers (the bigger the better), go to the library and read current travel magazines. Inquire about "companion" arrangements (e.g., U.S. Air flies companion with British Air, Air Canada and others) so you can take advantage of combination rate structures and frequent flyer mileage.

Ask about red-eye specials, companion-free or—discount offers. If there will be two or more flying, and staying over a Saturday. Flying to alternate airports can sometimes save money; fly/drive/hotel combinations are often available; weekend discounts are normally offered; and many airlines offer reduced fares for last-minute flights due to funerals or serious illness of family members. While you are making your inquiries, question how many seats are left on the flight at the price quoted.

Discounted tickets may be "non-refundable," although an unused ticket can often—for a fee—be exchanged. Get the details before you buy. Trip cancellation insurance is available if the expenditure is a major one, so comparison shop for that also. Consider hidden costs: food prices are normally inflated in airports; transportation costs from destination airport to ultimate destination; non-transfer of luggage; long tiring layovers that cost you a day of other activities while you recuperate; inconvenient arrival time, adding public transportation or hotel costs. The cheapest flight is not always the best bargain.

Make a chart of the results of your research so comparison will be easy. Your chart should include a column for booking and purchase dates. When you have decided on your flight, do a quick re-check the day prior to the booking date, as there may have been price cuts.

Flight pricing is an on-going war but you can benefit from it if you are willing to spend some time. A last note of caution: ask the travel agent and the airline about availability of flights. Flights to some destinations during certain times of the year fill rapidly, and waiting to book may result in cancellation of a once-in-a-lifetime opportunity. (Friends, a family of four, had to cancel a long-planned trip to Australia in July because they thought, if they waited to book flights, the price might come down. Instead, there were no seats available.) If your destination is overseas, consider tours which often offer better prices in a package than you can obtain on your own. Tours are not limited to the narrow guidelines depicted in the brochures; they normally allow travelers to join late, leave early, or add days or weeks

Leaving your automobile at the airport can also be a costly expense of your trip. Check nearby hotels and motels. Many offer parking at the hotel while you are gone and shuttle to and from the airport. The savings may be substantial.

Myths About Buying and Owning Vacation Property

By Mary S. Ludwig

While most people dream of owning a vacation home—a weekend house by the lake or perhaps a condo in a ski resort—most think that it's just out of their reach. Misconceptions abound when it comes to this topic. But we're here to set the record straight and show you that there is a change for many to make that dream come true.

Myth 1. Vacation homes are very expensive. Reality—some are. Prices for vacation homes run the gamut from very expensive to quite inexpensive. Many vacation areas have homes for sale for under— and in some cases significantly under--$100.00. Well-known examples include Cape Cod and the Hamptons.

Myth 2. Only the rich can afford vacation homes. Reality—only the rich can afford expensive vacation homes. A couple with $50,000 a year in income would be able to carry a total of $170,000 of debt. With a $100,000 mortgage on their primary home and no other outstanding debts, they'd qualify for a $70,000 mortgage on a vacation home. With a down payment of $30,000, a $100,000 vacation home could easily be theirs.

Myth 3. Financing is difficult to obtain for a vacation home. Reality—banks are anxious to lend to individuals with good credit and adequate income. In some cases, a bank will require a down payment of 30% of the purchase price for a vacation home, but 20% is adequate for most. And in some instances, especially when a developer has made special arrangements with a bank, 10% might do.

Myth 4. If you buy a vacation home, you will have to vacation in the same place every year. Reality—says who? If you want, you can always rent it or exchange the use of your vacation home for the use of someone else's in another part of the country or another country altogether.

Myth 5. Vacation homes make poor investments. Reality—short term that's probably true—but any real estate makes a lousy short term investment. Most who bought in the 70's or early to mid 80's made substantial profits. As baby boomers approach middle age (Ouch!)—the prime time for buying vacation home—the demand will undoubtedly increase, forcing prices upward again.

Myth 6. Tax reform killed all tax benefits related to owning a vacation home. Reality—only for the wealthy! This is one of the few tax advantages still left for the average American. Mortgage interest on one—and only one—second home remains deductible. And for those with incomes less than $100,000, losses up to $25,000 on rental property are deductible. So, if you rent your vacation home for part of the year….

Myth 7. If you treat your vacation home as a rental property, you can use it yourself only two weeks. Reality—this is only partially true. You can use your rental property for the greater of two weeks or 10% of the time it is rented. So, if you have a summer home which you rent for ten months of the year (say 300 days), you could use the house yourself for 30 days, not 14.

So, if you've always dreamed of owning your own little get away spot and thought it was out of reach, now might be the time to reconsider.

Improve Your Image (Without Spending a Fortune)

By Sheila O'Connor

Why is it that some women just seem to have the "look" of power and authority? Very often the secret is in the way they present themselves. Don't think you have that sort of money to spend on creating a professional or put together look? Then think again. Even during recessionary times, there are ways you can improve your image—whether for the home or the office—without going overboard on spending Susan Hilton of Beauticontrol in Washington D.C. says "Developing a polished image need not be an expensive or difficult process. Attention to little points can make a tremendous difference."

Here are some tips Susan recommends for ensuring you *always* look your best, even when your budget is at its worst.

- Always wear shoulder pads. These should be about half an inch thick. They will add height and width, making you look taller and more importantly, slimmer.

- Taper your skirts. Your skirt should be tapered between the hip and the knee to make you look slimmer. Keeping a skirt the same width as your widest part will just make you look wide everywhere.

- Use small squares of chiffon or silk as pocket handkerchiefs. You can pick these up at remnant sales. The splash of classy material will make you look elegant and chic.

- Wear a blazer over a dress or matching skirt and blouse. It adds instant authority.

- To look thinner and taller, wear a pin high up on the shoulder of your jacket.

- Wear earrings at least the size of a quarter. This will make you look slimmer as well as give you an air of confidence and draw attention to your eyes.

- Don't wear too much jewelry. Three pieces is the absolute maximum (earrings, chains, pins) but usually two is enough. Sometimes just wearing expensive looking earrings is sufficient.

- For a slimmer appearance, make sure your hosiery matches your skirt and/or the color of your shoes.

- For a professional office look, wear mid-heeled pumps, not open or sling-back styles.

- Use cosmetics to flatter your face and give the image that you care about the way you look.

- Wear the right colors for you. Even in a recession, have a consultation. The money you spend will be a lifetime investment in the way you look. Never again will you have to appear washed-out or even ill in colors that do nothing to flatter you. In fact, just wearing the right colors can actually make you look younger and slimmer all on its own!

- Have an annual "clear out" of all the clothes that you haven't worn in the last two months. Give them away to a friend or charity. Treat yourself to a new flattering outfit now that you have some clear space to put it in (even yard sale clothes can look good if they are the right color, and they won't be expensive).

- Keep a professional image by cleaning your shoes regularly. Don't spoil all your extra efforts on the above tips then ruin them by having scuffed shoes.

- If you must wear fragrance (in surveys, most office workers prefer their colleagues not to wear any) keep it light and subtle. Don't allow your scent to arrive before you do. Since your body will get used to it, you might not notice when you are wearing too much, so ask a friend or colleague to let you know.

- Always keep hands and nails in good condition. You'd be surprised how often your hands are in view and un-manicured or bitten nails are easily spotted.

Keeping your image in tip top condition need not be expensive or difficult and the results are always sure to get you noticed!

www.ingramcontent.com/pod-product-compliance
Lightning Source LLC
Chambersburg PA
CBHW051341170526
45166CB00002B/912